Collecting Passions

Collecting

Discovering the Fun of
Stamps and Other Stuff From
All Over the Place

Canadian Museum
of Civilization

Musée Canadien
des Civilisations

CANADIAN POSTAL MUSEUM
MUSÉE CANADIEN DE LA POSTE

KPk
Key Porter Kids

Passions

By Susan McLeod O'Reilly

Activities by Alain Massé

Illustrations by Norman Eyolfson

For Luke. – Susan McLeod O'Reilly

Text copyright © 1999 by Canadian Museum of Civilization. Illustrations copyright ©1999 by Norman Eyolfson

Canadian Cataloguing in Publication Data

McLeod O'Reilly, Susan, 1955-
Collecting passions : discovering the fun of stamps and other stuff from all over the place,
co-published by the Canadian Museum of Civilization
ISBN 1-55013-676-3

1. Stamp collecting – Juvenile literature. I. Massé, Alain, 1958- .
II. Eyolfson, Norman. III. Canadian Museum of Civilization
IV. Title

HE6213.M35 1999   769.56'075   C95-930267-0

We acknowledge the financial support of the Government of Canada through the
Book Publishing Industry Development Program (BPIDP) for our publishing activities.

The publisher gratefully acknowledges the support of the
Canada Council for the Arts and the Ontario Arts Council for its publishing program.

Key Porter kids is an imprint of
Key Porter Books Limited
70 The Esplanade, Toronto, Ontario
Canada M5E 1R2
www.keyporter.com

Design: Jean Lightfoot Peters

Printed and bound in Hong Kong (China)

00 01 02 6 5 4 3 2 1

DO YOU COLLECT?

Almost everyone collects something. Some people collect things of great value, such as antique cars. Many just collect items that are fun to look at, like rocks, buttons or bottle caps. Not everything we collect can be displayed. Some people collect stories, songs or jokes. Other people collect things they think may be of value one day, such as sports cards.

What would you like to collect? Think of things that represent your world. Chances are it's those things that will be of value one day. There's a catch: you must keep your collection in perfect condition. It's not enough to collect neat stuff and dump it in a drawer.

Collecting Passions

Look around this bedroom.

- Using a magnifying glass, look for collections of sports cards, soaps, hairclips, rocks, stuffed animals and postage stamps.

- Can you find any other collections? How many collections are there altogether?

- Now look around your own bedroom. What collections do you have?

Match the Collector to His or Her Collection

Match the collector to their hobby. You might want to ask family members to help you. (Answers are at the back of the book.)

aerophilately — the collecting of postage stamps

cartophily — the collecting of cards (baseball, hockey, etc.)

phillumeny — the collecting of cheese labels

militaria — the collecting of matchbooks and matchbox labels

hostelaphily — the collecting of bank notes

laclabphily — the collecting of objects used by the military

philately — the collecting of airmail stamps

conchology — the collecting of outdoor signs from inns

discophily — the collecting of dolls

planganology — the collecting of records

notaphily — the collecting of sea shells

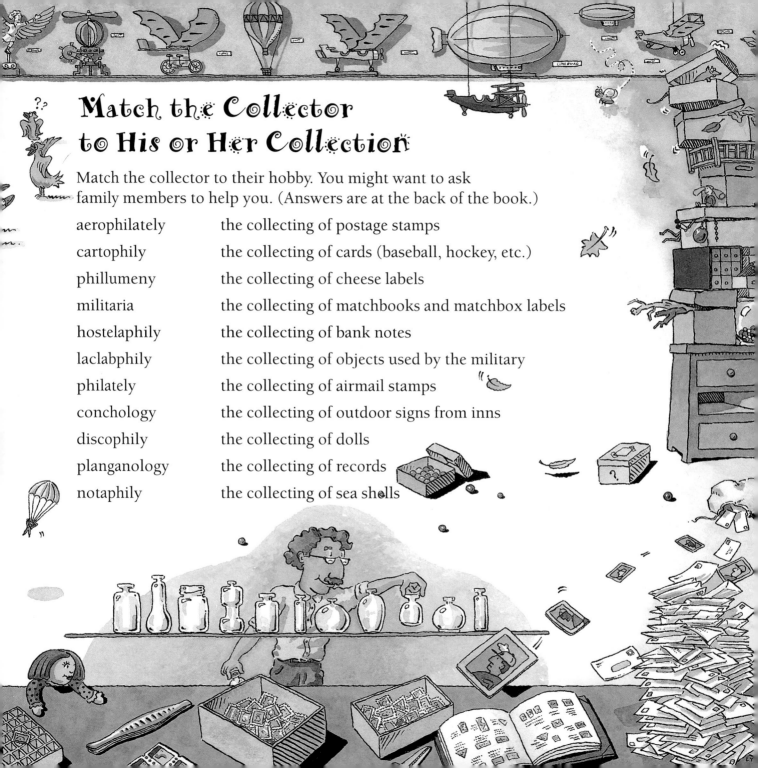

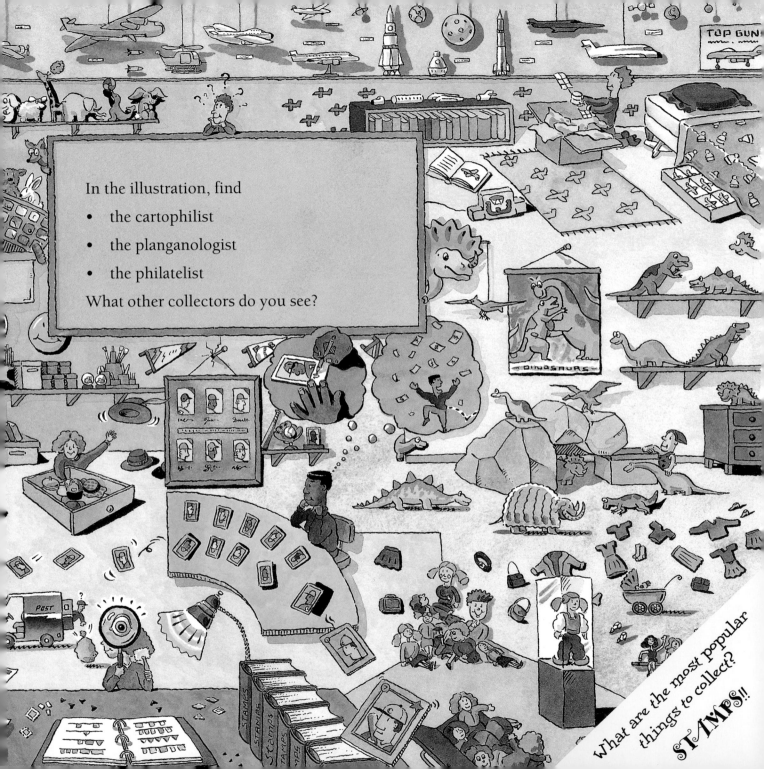

In the illustration, find

- the cartophilist
- the planganologist
- the philatelist

What other collectors do you see?

What are the most popular things to collect? STAMPS!!

TOP GUN

DINOSAURS

POST

STAMPS
STAMPS
STAMPS
STAMPS

Why are stamp collections so popular?

- No matter what part of the world you live in, everyone uses postage stamps.
- Stamps are free. By removing the stamps from the envelopes you receive in the mail, you can have a collection without spending anything.
- Stamps are educational. The pictures on stamps can tell you a lot about the country that printed them.
- Stamps fit into tiny spaces.
- Stamps are potentially valuable.
- Stamp collectors make good friends. Collectors gather at stamp fairs, talk on the Internet and meet at clubs. Many kid collectors even help other kids with their collections by giving or trading stamps.

SEND A STAMP

Why waste a stamp? Attach a postcard to it. Take a postcard-sized piece of cardboard and glue a snapshot to it or draw a picture. On the flip side, put a stamp on the right-hand corner, write your pal's address and drop it in the post. Don't forget to write a message or a joke!

DID YOU KNOW that Great Britain is the only country that doesn't put its name on postage stamps? Instead there is a drawing of the queen (or king).

The First Messages

Before there were stamps, or letters, or written words, there was — shouting! Shouting wasn't the best way to get a message across, so messengers came into being. In Ancient Greece these messengers were super fit runners who, as the myth goes, ran so fast they barely left footprints in the sand. It is because of these messengers that the marathon is a highlight of the Olympic Games.

Most Greek, and later Roman, messengers were slaves. A slave could gossip or be robbed, so some masters shaved their slave's hair and wrote on the bald head. Not only could the slave not see the top of his head, chances were he couldn't read. As the slave ran to his destination, the words disappeared under growing hair. When he arrived, his head was shaved again and the message read.

DID YOU KNOW that the first recorded mail route was in ancient China? The messengers, called relay riders, carried mail and ran up to 70 miles (112 kilometers) a day.

MAKE A SKYTALE

Want to send a secret message to a friend the way Spartan military leaders did? Take two sticks of identical width and length. These are called skytales. Have your friend take one stick. Each of you draws a starting line at the bottom of your stick. Wind a long strip of paper around your skytale (the Spartans used papyrus leaves). Write your message across the paper, along the stick. You can write two or three lines. Unwind the paper and send it to your friend. To decipher the message your friend must wind the paper around their skytale.

The Age of the Stamp

The invention of stamps changed all our lives.
Not only was it easier for people to keep in touch,
it also encouraged them to learn to read and write.
All this was thanks to an Englishman named Rowland Hill.

As the story goes, and it may not be entirely true,
Rowland Hill (1795-1879) was at his second home in
Scotland when a letter came for one of his servants.
The servant-girl took it from the delivery man, examined it,
handed it back and went about her work. In those days
the recipient of a letter had to pay the postage. Mr. Hill
was a kind-hearted gent, and thinking the girl could not
afford the postage, he paid it. Imagine his surprise when
the girl scolded him for wasting his money. Why?

It seems there was no letter in the envelope. The servant-
girl and her brother had a code: if he marked the envelope
one way, it meant he was well; if it was marked another
way, it showed he was unhappy or in trouble. From this, Mr.
Hill came up with the idea of creating small labels to stick
to envelopes to show the postage had been paid. When
other countries learned about this idea, they too started
making postage stamps.

DID YOU KNOW that before envelopes were invented, people folded their letters and sealed them with wax? The more sheets of paper in the letter, the more it cost to be mailed.

The First Stamps

The Penny Black, issued in Great Britain in 1840, was the world's first stamp with sticky gum on the back. A million of these stamps were printed and, although it's not especially rare, many collectors think it's neat to have one in their collection. This stamp didn't stay around, though, because the stamp was so dark the cancelation mark couldn't be seen.

The Twopenny Blue also came in 1840 and lasted for forty years. Both the Penny Blacks and the Twopenny Blues had to be cut apart with scissors (until 1854 when the perforating machine was introduced), so many of these stamps were slightly damaged. There were three different versions of this stamp, but it's the first version that's the most valuable.

The Penny Red (which in fact looks brown) replaced the Penny Black. It stayed in circulation, with a few minor changes, until 1880.

You only need a bit of paint!

MAKE YOUR OWN STAMPS

Personalized stamps have made a comeback. Here's a way to make your own.

Potato Cut-Up

You will need:

- 2 or more raw potatoes or apples
- 1 sharp knife (an Exacto knife works best)*
- liquid tempera paint in wide-mouth bowls (2 or more colors)
- newspaper
- envelopes (optional)

Cut the raw potato (or apple) in half. With a knife, carve your initials into it. Remember: it's the protruding marks that leave an imprint. Dip the carved end of the potato into the paint. Practice making stamps on the newspaper. Put your stamps onto the envelopes.

*You will need your parents' permission before working with a knife. Parents: teach your child *to cut away* from themselves and be on hand to supervise.

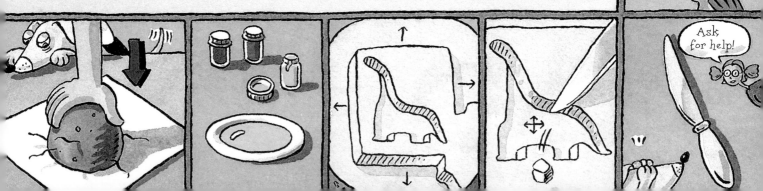

The Mail Must Get Through!

Delivery can often be difficult. Every possible way to carry the mail is considered. The boy in this picture wants to send a letter to his grandmother, but the messengers won't always co-operate. Draw a path that gets his letter through!

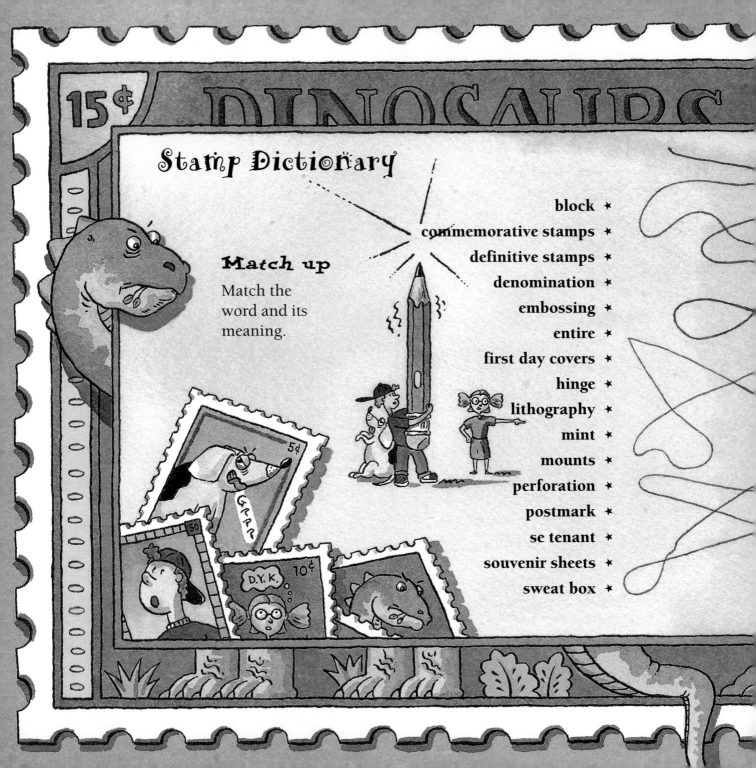

Stamp Dictionary

Match up

Match the word and its meaning.

block ★
commemorative stamps ★
definitive stamps ★
denomination ★
embossing ★
entire ★
first day covers ★
hinge ★
lithography ★
mint ★
mounts ★
perforation ★
postmark ★
se tenant ★
souvenir sheets ★
sweat box ★

Answers are at the back of the book.

* cancelation of stamp on the envelope
* box with lid, removes hinges or paper from stamps
* a stamp that has never been used
* stamps issued to honor a person or event
* four or more stamps taken from a sheet of stamps
* plastic holders used to protect stamps
* common stamps
* stamp and envelope with original letter inside
* stamps with commemorative inscriptions
* the process of printing stamps using a flat plate
* envelopes with stamps canceled on the day of issue
* paper that attaches the stamp to the album
* the cost of the stamp printed on the stamp
* jagged edges around the stamp
* a stamp produced by pressing a design onto paper
* different stamps printed side by side

Stamps from Around the World

How can you travel the world but not leave home?
You can collect stamps from different countries.
Through the pictures you can:

- ✷ visit the Emperor of Japan
- ✷ play drums in an English band
- ✷ climb a tree in the rainforests of Brazil
- ✷ wrestle a panda bear in China
- ✷ climb Mount Everest in Nepal
- ✷ play soccer in Italy
- ✷ shake hands with a dinosaur in Canada
- ✷ tickle a snake in India
- ✷ float in a hot air balloon over the castles of France
- ✷ ride a camel in Egypt
- ✷ swim with dolphins off the Fiji Islands
- ✷ chase a kangaroo in Australia

The Envelope Please!

If you like to solve mysteries, why not study the strange markings on envelopes? The post office puts secret messages on them. Can you break the code? Using a magnifying glass, try and decipher some of these:

- ✉ the date and place of mailing: when was the letter mailed and where was it sent from?

- ✉ the cancelation: what design did the post office mark on the stamp to stop it from being used again? Over the years, these designs have changed a lot.

- ✉ the cost: how much did the post office charge to deliver the letter? Compare two envelopes from different years. Do you see a big difference in cost?

- ✉ the transportation: was a train, ship, airplane or hot air balloon used to carry the letter?

- ✉ the postal code: did a machine cancel and sort the envelope? **Hint:** look for rows of dots sprayed next to the address.

- ✉ postage stamps: when was the stamp printed or issued? **Hint:** find the date marked on each Canadian stamp since 1974.

Don't forget to put your return address.

Your postal code is converted to machine-readable language.

DID YOU KNOW that some stamps have watermarks on them to prevent forgery? The marks are pressed into paper with tiny bits of metal arranged in patterns. Hold a stamp up to the light and spot the watermark.

25¢

Stamps With Mistakes

If you want to collect something really unusual, you could collect postage stamps with mistakes! Thousands of copies of a stamp are printed at the same time, and sometimes mistakes are made on some, or all, copies. If only a few of these "different" stamps exist, they can be worth a lot of money. How can two stamps look the same but be different?

picture   A mistake can happen when the picture is printed. You may have to use a magnifying glass to find the mistake.

color   The wrong color ink may have been used.

paper   Some stamps may have been printed on a different kind of paper.

perforations   The bumpy edge around a stamp is called the perforation. This bumpy edge may look different on one of the stamps.

If you have a lot of copies of a stamp, look for differences among them. Since differences among stamps of the same design are rare and usually hard to see, a collection of these stamps is difficult to build.

Look closely.

DID YOU KNOW you can use a perforation gauge and an ultraviolet light to spot watermarks and mistakes?

Looking for the Post Office's Mistakes

To find mistakes or flaws, you have to look very closely. Look through a magnifying glass and find the mistakes. How many errors can you find?

Let's Begin Collecting

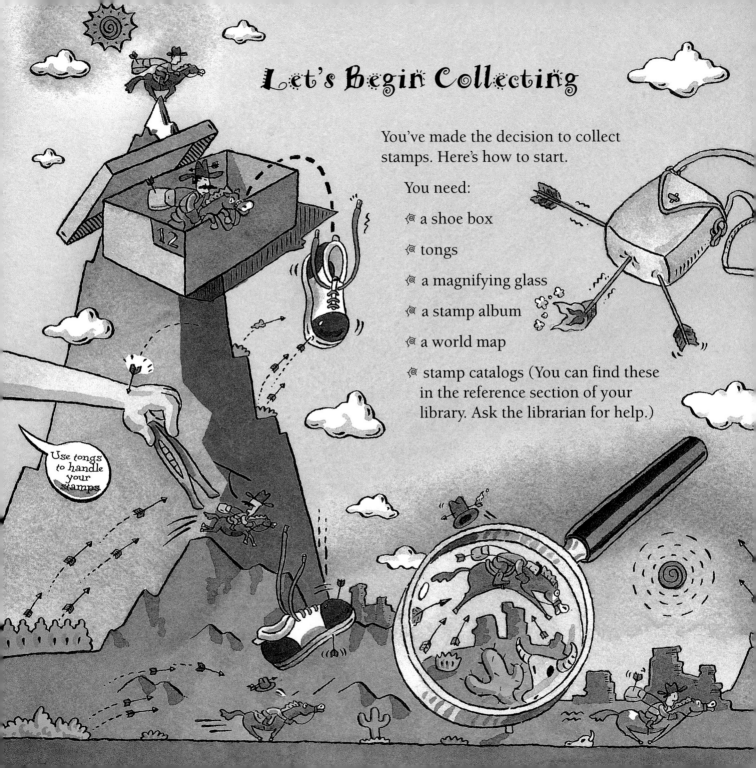

You've made the decision to collect stamps. Here's how to start.

You need:

- a shoe box
- tongs
- a magnifying glass
- a stamp album
- a world map
- stamp catalogs (You can find these in the reference section of your library. Ask the librarian for help.)

Use tongs to handle your stamps

The Hunt

The easiest way to begin is to buy a junior stamp collector's kit. It will come with a packet of stamps. Next you can buy your own stamps. They come in two classes: mixed or all different. Mixed, or mixtures, contain duplicate stamps with cancelation marks. All-different packages contain only one copy of each stamp. Use these stamps to start, but don't stop there:

1. Ask friends and relatives to send you canceled stamps and envelopes.
2. Pop into a local business and ask to have their canceled stamps. To collect foreign stamps, ask companies that deal with foreign countries.
3. Ask your post office for information on stamp collecting.
4. Use the phone book to find stamp dealers and stores.

DID YOU KNOW that long before the Wright Brothers' Flyer took to the sky, messages were carried by air? As early as Roman times, people strapped messages to pigeons. This came to be called a pigeongram.

TIP: One boy handed dozens of self-addressed postcards to a friend of his father's who traveled the world regularly. The traveler bought stamps at the various hotels he visited and simply mailed the postcards back to the boy. The boy managed to collect a stunning range of stamps from all around the world.

Choosing an Album

Albums protect and display stamps. Choose one with heavy bond paper and three-hole punches. You may prefer illustrated pages; it can be fun looking for stamps to fit into the squares (or frustrating, if the stamps can't be found). Remember: store your album in an upright position in a cool, dry place.

DID YOU KNOW that in Tonga, South Pacific, the mail was put in biscuit tins and tossed overboard? Swimmers would catch the tins and bring them to shore. This is how the Tin Can Canoe Mail service began. The service ended when the volcano on the island erupted.

Pop Quiz

Think you know your stamp trivia? Careful, this is tough stuff! (Feel free to go through the book before checking your answers on the next page.)

1. What is the number one hobby in the world?

2. What is a stamp collector called?

3. Name a famous rider with the Pony Express.

4. How did Parisians get mail out of the city during the Siege of Paris in 1870?

5. What is a collector of bank notes called?

6. Who invented the stamp and what country did he come from?

7. What country does not put its name on its stamps?

8. How many countries in the world issue postage stamps?

9. Where was the first recorded mail route?

10. What were the first recorded mail route messengers in ancient China called?

How many did you get right?

9+ A stamp champ
7+ A stamp keener
5+ In six months you'll be a stamp whiz
2+ Hey, you're trying. What more can we ask?

Answers to
Match the Collector to His or Her Collection

notaphily	the collecting of bank notes
planganology	the collecting of dolls
discophily	the collecting of records
conchology	the collecting of sea shells
philately	the collecting of postage stamps
laclabphily	the collecting of cheese labels
hostelaphily	the collecting of outdoor signs from inns
militaria	the collecting of objects used by the military
phillumeny	the collecting of matchbooks and matchbox labels
cartophily	the collecting of cards (baseball, hockey, etc.)
aerophilately	the collecting of airmail stamps

Answers to Pop Quiz

1. Stamp collecting
2. Philatelist
3. William F. Cody, Buffalo Bill
4. Mail was put into steel balls and thrown into the river Seine
5. A notaphilist
6. Rowland Hill, Great Britain
7. Great Britain
8. 200
9. Ancient China
10. *Tshien-fu* or strong men

Answers to Stamp Dictionary

block — four or more stamps taken from a sheet of stamps

commemorative stamp — stamps issued to honor a person or event

definitive stamps — common stamps

denomination —the cost of the stamp printed on the stamp

embossing — a stamp produced by pressing a design onto paper

entire — stamp and envelope with original letter inside

first day covers — envelopes with stamps canceled on the day of issue

hinge — paper that attaches the stamp to the album

lithography — the process of printing stamps using a flat plate

mint — a stamp that has never been used

mounts — plastic holders used to protect stamps

perforation — jagged edges around the stamp

postmark — cancelation of stamp on the envelope

se tenant — different stamps printed side by side

souvenir sheets — stamps with commemorative inscriptions

sweat box — box with lid, removes hinges or paper from stamps

Addresses of Stamp Clubs for Children

Starting a stamp collection is a great idea. Here is a list of a few places that can help you either start on the road to your collection, join a stamp collecting club, or just get more information on stamp collecting.

STAMP QUEST
National Philatelic Centre
Canada Post
75 St. Ninian Street
Antigonish, NS
B2G 2R8 Canada
or call toll-free 1-800-565-CLUB
(in Canada)

STAMP HUNTER CLUB
Stamps Business Unit
New Zealand Post Limited
7-27 Waterloo Quay
Wellington, New Zealand

STAMP EXPLORER
P.O. Box 511
South Melbourne, Victoria 3205
Australia

STAMPERS
Stampers Cool-lectibles
US Postal Service
P.O. Box 419636
Kansas City, MO 64141-6636
USA
or call toll-free Stamp-Fun (in the USA)

VOYAGER STAMP GANG
An Post
General Post Office
O'Connell Street
Dublin 1
Ireland

The Philatelic Internet

If you have a computer it's also a good idea to see what's available through the Internet. One great website for kids interested in stamp collecting is called Stamps 4 Kids. You can find it at:

www.bumperland.com

This website features activities that promote stamp collecting for kids, answers questions and provides you with all kinds of great information, right at your fingertips!

Also check out the following:

Junior Philatelists on the Internet
www.ioa.com/~ggayland/junior

Junior Philatelists of America
www.jpastamps.org

Youth Collectors Zone
www.stamps-auctions.com

Stamp Quest
www.stampquest.com

Canadian Postal Museum
www.civilization.ca

Stamp Collectors for Beginners
www.geocities.com/Heartland/2769

Philately
www.geocities.com/Heartland/Plains/1466

Stamp Collecting Site for Kids
www.karoo.net/wilcom

0/1 $^1/_{02}$ 4-4-05